Written by Noah Leatherland

FOOTBALL

Published in 2025
by The Rosen Publishing Group, Inc.
2544 Clinton Street, Buffalo, NY 14224

© 2024 BookLife Publishing Ltd.

Written by: Noah Leatherland
Edited by: E.C. Andrews
Designed by: Jasmine Pointer

Cataloging-in-Publication Data

Names: Leatherland, Noah, 1999-.
Title: Football / Noah Leatherland.
Description: Buffalo, NY : PowerKids Press, 2025. | Series: World of sports | Includes glossary and index.
Identifiers: ISBN 9781499448986 (pbk.) | ISBN 9781499448993 (library bound) | ISBN 9781499449006 (ebook)
Subjects: LCSH: Football--Juvenile literature.
Classification: LCC GV950.7 L384 2025 | DDC 796.332--dc23

Manufactured in the United States of America

CPSIA Compliance Information: Batch #CW25PK. For further information contact Rosen Publishing at 1-800-237-9932.

Find us on 📘 📷

IMAGE CREDITS

All images are courtesy of Shutterstock.com. With thanks to Getty Images, Thinkstock Photo and iStockphoto.

Cover – Eugene Onischenko, Akito Studio, Alice July, je48design. Throughout – je48design. 4–5 – Brocreative, Kim Reinick. 6–7 – Jamie Lamor Thompson, Richard Paul Kane. 8–9 – shocky, JoeSAPhotos. 10–11 – Ken Durden, Steve Jacobson. 12–13 – Alexey Stiop, Ringo Chiu. 14–15 – Ruth Peterkin, Debby Wong. 16–17 – Andrey_Popov, Richard Paul Kane. 18–19 – Richard Paul Kane, Brocreative. 20–21 – Jai Agnish, Alena Veasey. 22–23 – Alex Kravtsov, SUSAN LEGGETT, threerocksimages.

CONTENTS

WORDS THAT LOOK LIKE THIS CAN BE FOUND IN THE GLOSSARY ON PAGE 24.

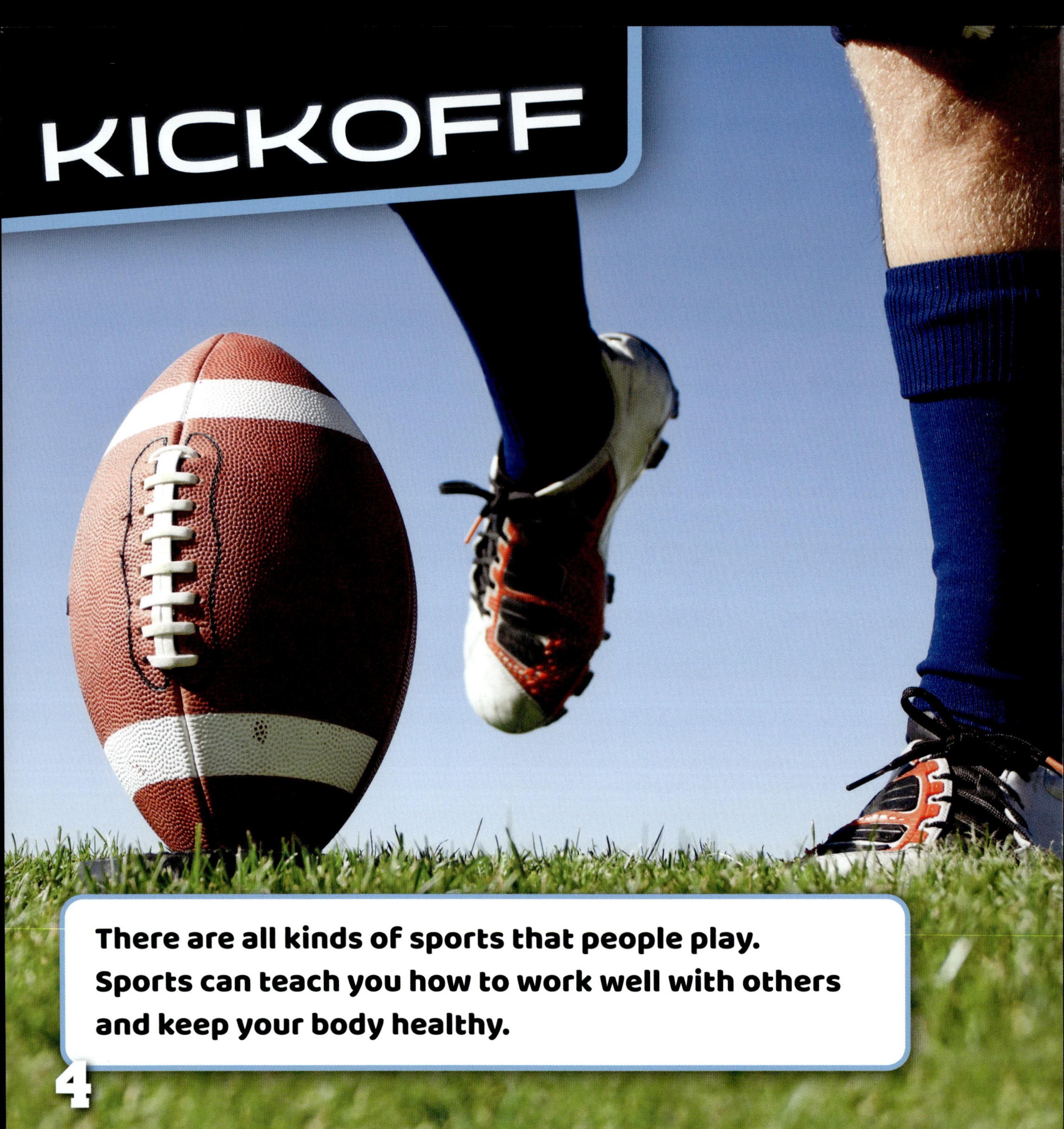

There are all kinds of sports that people play. Sports can teach you how to work well with others and keep your body healthy.

Football is a sport that involves a lot of throwing, catching, running, tackling, and kicking. It seems simple. However, there are a lot of things that the players have to think about.

THE BASICS

A game of football has four quarters. Each quarter lasts for 15 minutes. Each team has 11 players on the field. Teams change who is on the field depending on what is happening.

In football, teams mainly score points by getting the football into an <u>opponent</u>'s end zone. The ball can be moved forward by throwing it, running with it, or kicking it.

When a team has <u>possession</u> of the football, they are on offense. Teams on offense have four tries to move the ball forward 10 <u>yards</u>. These tries are called downs.

The playing field between each team's end zone is 100 yards long.

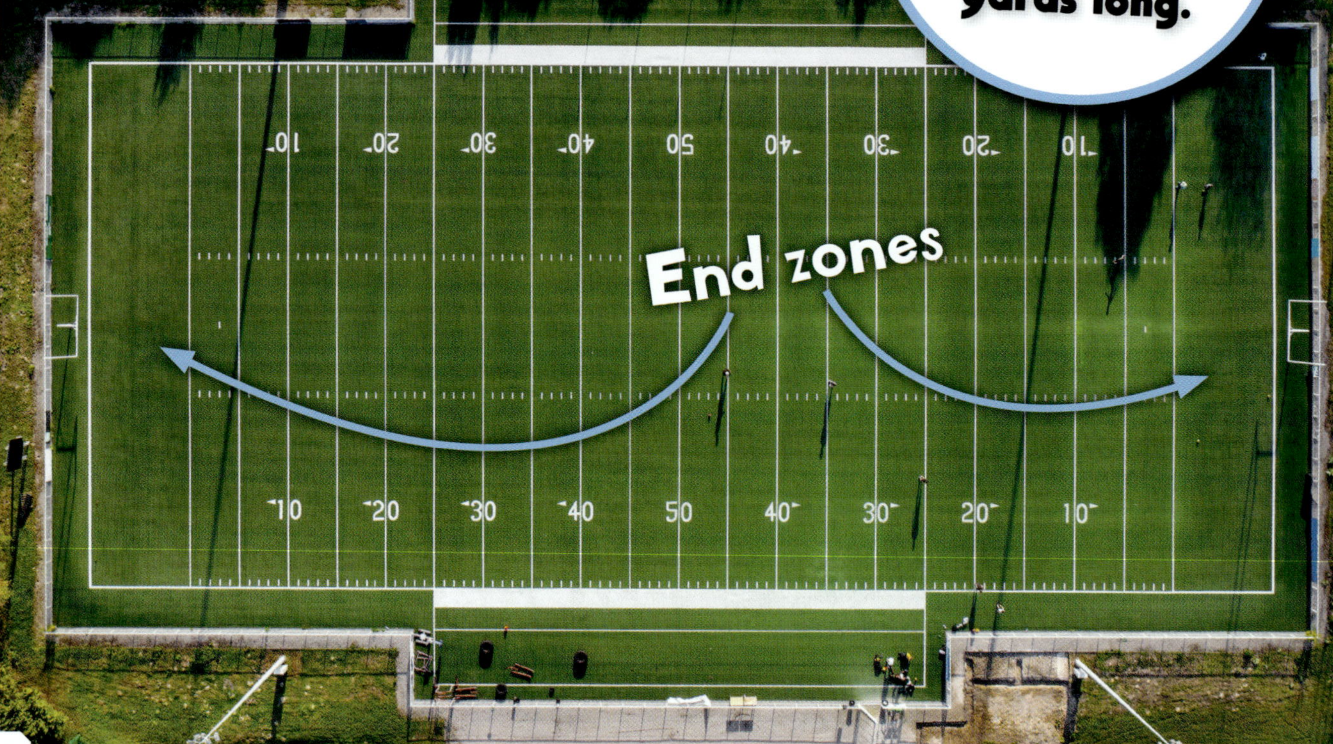

After moving the ball 10 yards, the offensive team starts again on a first down. If they have not moved the ball 10 yards after their fourth down, their opponents gain possession of the ball.

OFFENSIVE POSITIONS

Plays start when the center gives the ball to the quarterback. The center is part of the offensive line. The offensive line also includes players called guards and tackles.

Quarterbacks usually pass the ball or hand it to another player. Players called wide receivers and tight ends run to catch a quarterback's pass. Running backs get handed the ball to run with.

DEFENSIVE POSITIONS

Players on defense are trying to stop their opponents from moving the ball forward. The defensive line is made up of players called tackles and ends. They try to stop the offensive plays early on.

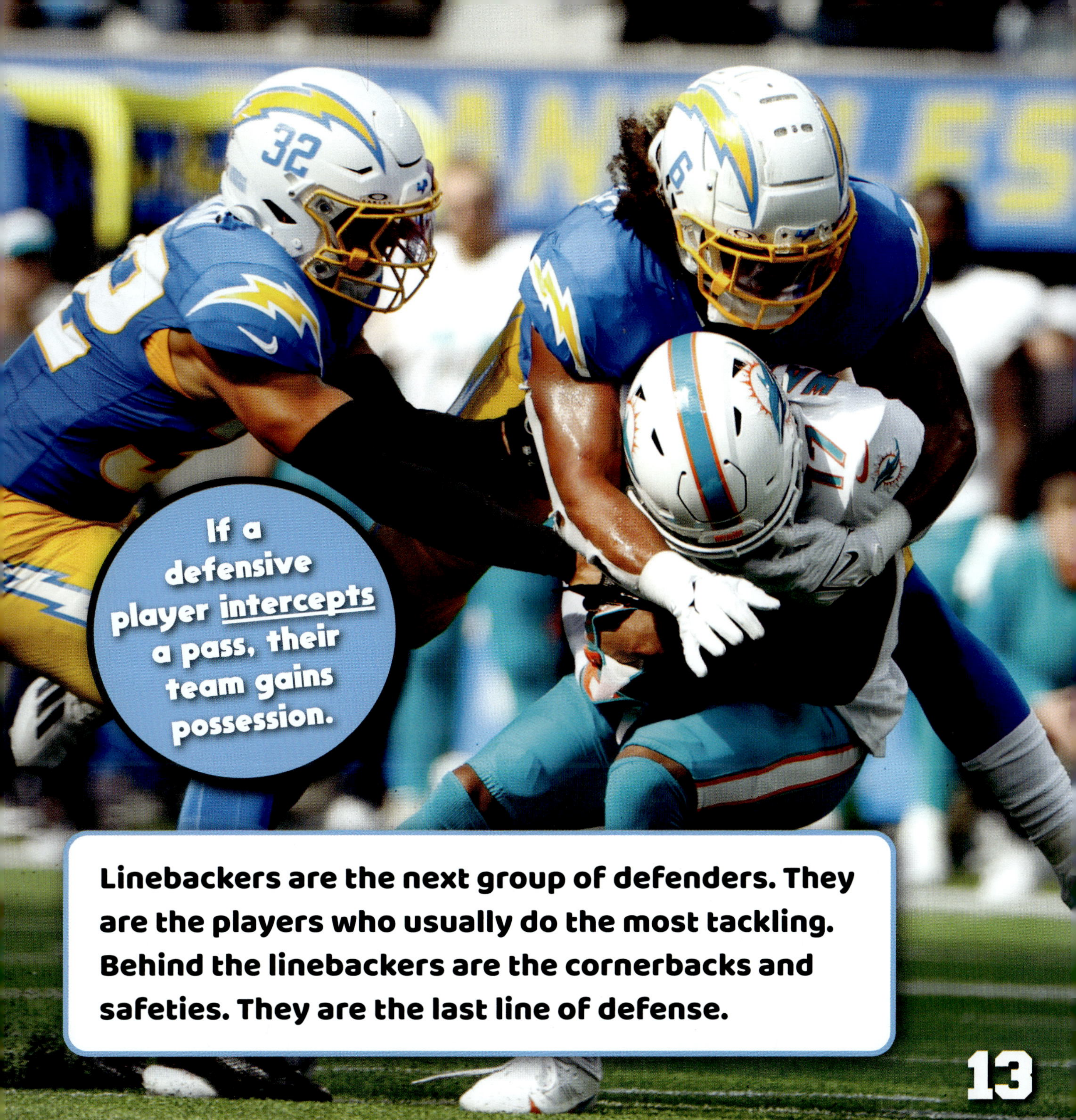

Linebackers are the next group of defenders. They are the players who usually do the most tackling. Behind the linebackers are the cornerbacks and safeties. They are the last line of defense.

SPECIAL TEAMS POSITIONS

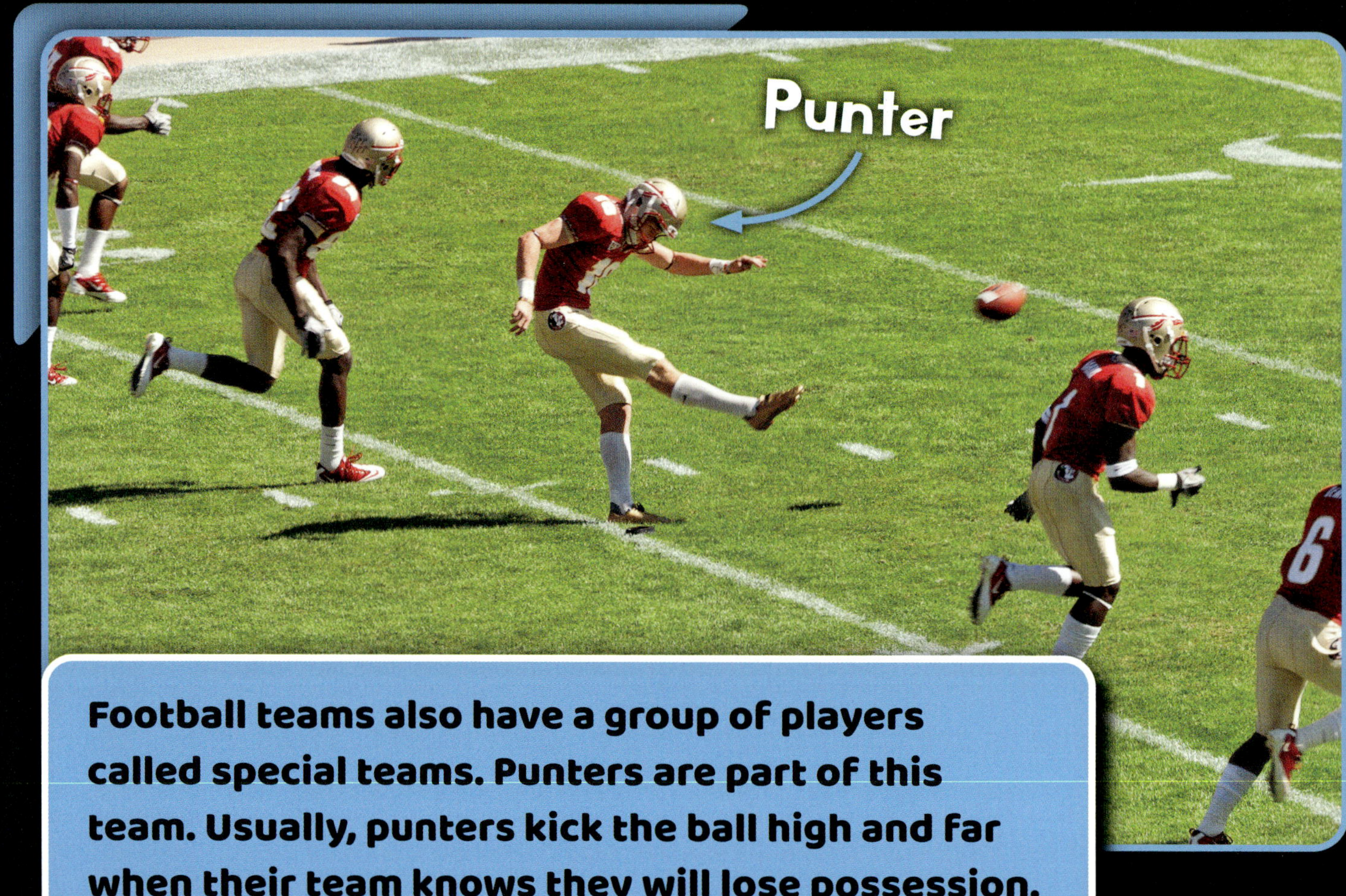

Football teams also have a group of players called special teams. Punters are part of this team. Usually, punters kick the ball high and far when their team knows they will lose possession.

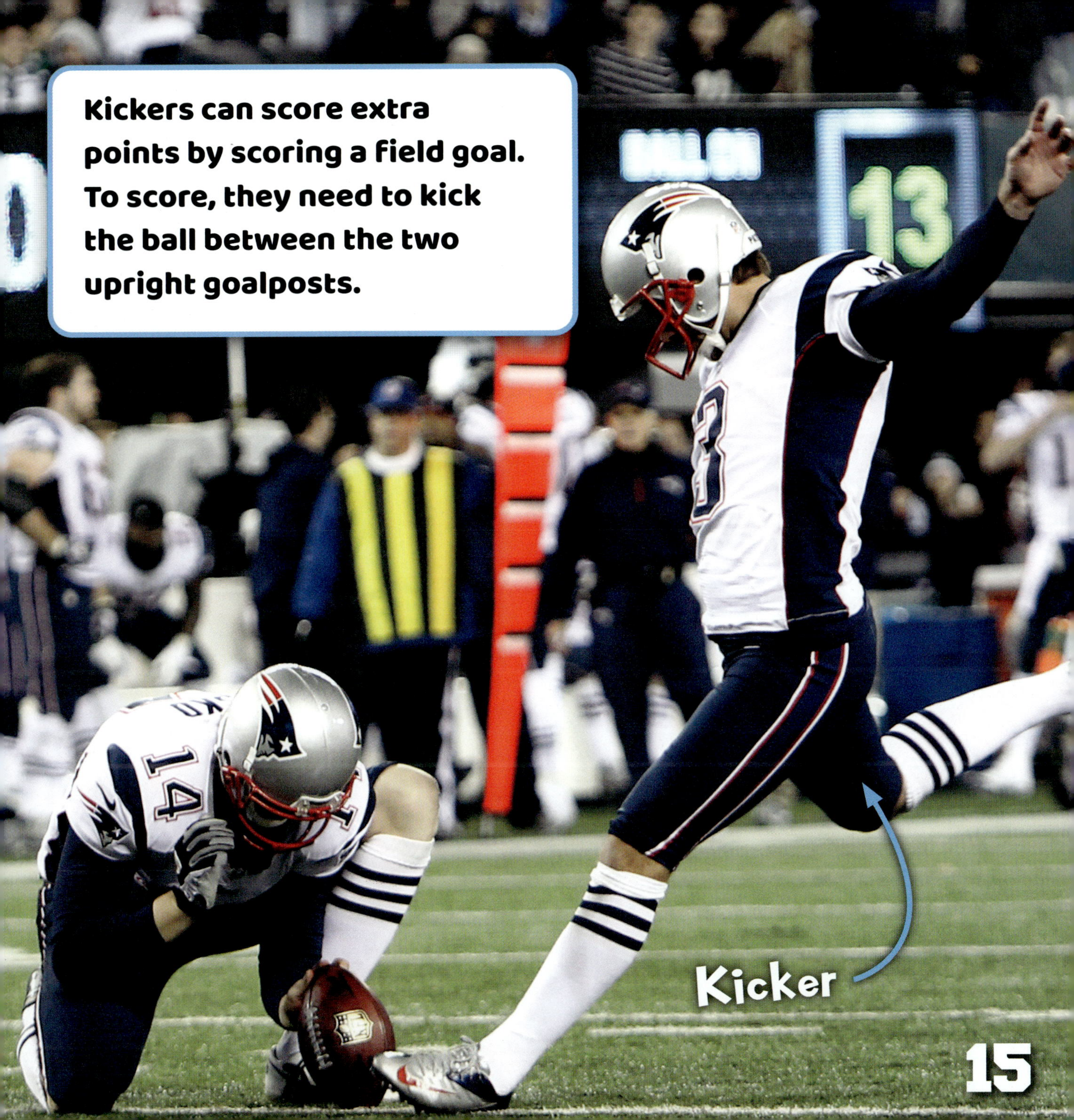

Kickers can score extra points by scoring a field goal. To score, they need to kick the ball between the two upright goalposts.

13

14

Kicker

TACTICS

Tactics are a very big part of football. Coaches teach their players different plays. Quarterbacks shout secret phrases to tell their team what play they are going for. This is called their cadence.

Teams also have different tactics when they defend. Teams can change the <u>formation</u> of their defense. Teams might play with more linebackers or with more players in their defensive line.

FOULS

Football has a lot of rules to follow. If players break one of these rules, it is called a foul. Fouls include players not being in the right place or playing dangerously.

Referee

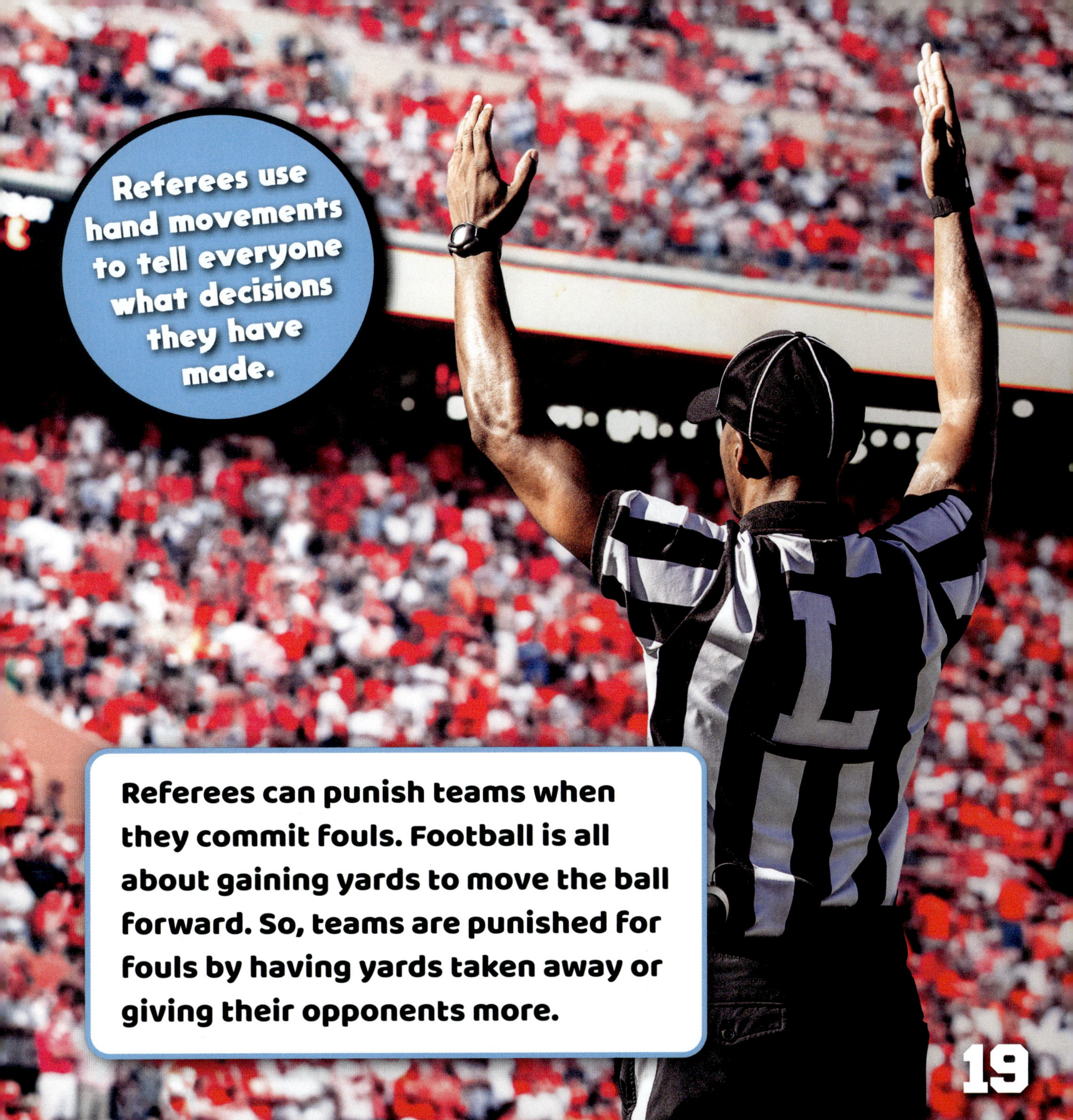

Referees can punish teams when they commit fouls. Football is all about gaining yards to move the ball forward. So, teams are punished for fouls by having yards taken away or giving their opponents more.

THE SUPER BOWL

The Super Bowl is the biggest football game of the year. It brings thousands of fans to massive stadiums and millions of people watch it on TV all around the world.

The first Super Bowl took place in 1967. Vince Lombardi was the first coach to win the Super Bowl. Today, the trophy given out to the winners is called the Vince Lombardi Trophy.

Football has fans all over the world. Many people have a favorite team that they cheer on. Do you have a favorite football team? Do you have a favorite player?

Lots of people like to play football. They might play for their school, a local team, or just in the park with their friends. Go get on the field!

GLOSSARY

formation	where a team puts its players on the field
intercept	to catch something before it can reach its target
opponent	a player on the team one is playing against. Also, the team being played against.
phrase	short group of words with a meaning
play	plan for how players will move and act
possession	when one team has control of the ball
tactics	planned ways of doing something
yards	a unit of measurement that is 3 feet (0.9 m) long

INDEX